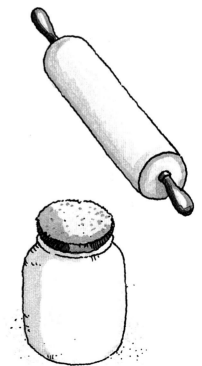

Copyright © 1998 Zero to Ten Ltd
Text copyright © 1996 Hannah Roche
Illustrations copyright © 1996 Chris Fisher

Edited by Anna McQuinn and Ambreen Husain
Designed by Suzy McGrath and Sarah Godwin

First published in Great Britain in 1996
by DeAgostini Editions.
First paperback edition published in 1998
by Zero to Ten Ltd
46 Chalvey Road East, Slough, Berkshire, SL1 2LR

A CIP catalogue record for this book
is available from the British Library.

ISBN 1-84089 044-4

Printed and bound in Spain

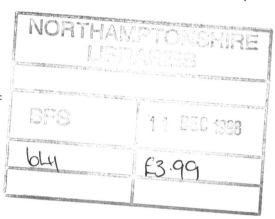
Food Science Consultant
Marianne Godwin

For Alice, CF

My Gran is GREAT!

Written by

Hannah Roche

Illustrated by

Chris Fisher

My gran is great!

Today she mixed some sugar and butter in a bowl – first it was grainy, but she kept beating until it was nice and smooth.

I mixed some flour, baking soda, salt and spices in another bowl – it was great fun!

Next Gran mixed together some golden
syrup and water. Then, little by little,
she added this and the flour
to the buttery mix.

When it got really stretchy,
Gran made it into a ball and
put it in the fridge. She said
that would make it less sticky.

After an hour, she took it out again.
She sprinkled flour all over the table
and put the fat ball of dough on top.

We got a rolling pin and we rolled and rolled.
The fat ball of dough got flatter and flatter,
thinner and thinner,
and wider and wider.

My gran is great!

Then I got my pastry cutter and cut
lots of little circles out of the dough.

Next I made two little men
and Gran made a little woman.

Then we made three dogs and a cow!

We put on some raisins for the eyes,
and cherries for the mouths.

Then Gran put them in the oven.
"Don't touch the oven," she said,
"it's hot!"

Abracadabra!
They had turned into **biscuits!**
You should let them cool down
but I sneaked one while
they were still warm.

It was lovely
and crispy
and a little
bit crumbly!

I love my gran.
She's great!

Yum!

Notes for Parents

EVEN very young children are aware that water is wet, rock is hard, sand is grainy. As they observe more, children discover that things don't always stay the same – rolling, heating, mixing, freezing and so on make things change from soft to hard, from round to flat, from liquid to solid...

LEARNING to notice and describe the textures and changes is important to children's understanding of the world around them. Don't worry about using 'proper' scientific words – getting the description right is what really matters.

YOU can recreate the story in your own kitchen by following the recipe opposite. As you go along, encourage your child to talk about what's happening. Then, you can eat the results!

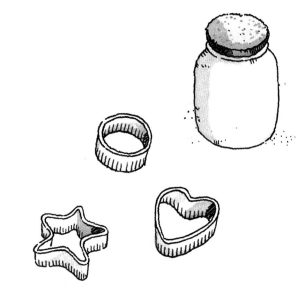

HOW IT WORKS

AS YOU mix the ingredients to make the dough, the butter gets softer and melts. If you rolled out the dough at this stage, it would be too soft and sticky.

PUTTING the dough in the fridge will make it stiff again. It's tricky to get it just right – if it's too cold it will crack around the edges, so you may have to let it sit for a few minutes before you roll it out.

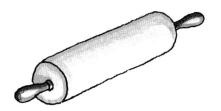

Millie's Recipe

YOU WILL NEED:

500 grams of flour
½ teaspoon of baking soda
½ teaspoon of salt
1 level teaspoon of ground ginger
¼ teaspoon of ground nutmeg
⅛ teaspoon of ground allspice
100 grams of sugar
100 grams of butter
8 tablespoons of golden syrup
currants and raisins for the eyes
cherries for the mouths
bowls, a whisk or electric mixer,
a rolling pin, grease-proof paper or
cling film, pastry cutters, a baking
tray, spoons for mixing, teaspoons,
a tablespoon and a wire rack

HINTS

MAKING the dough into a ball and
then pressing it into a disc before
refrigerating makes it easier to roll out.

1. Stir together the flour, baking soda,
   salt and spices. Mix well.
2. In a large bowl, beat together the butter
   and sugar until light and creamy.
3. Gradually add the golden syrup and
   the flour mixture to the butter and sugar.
4. Beat together until all the ingredients
   are combined, but do not overmix.
5. Gather the dough into a ball, press it into
   a disc, wrap it in grease-proof paper or
   cling film and chill it in the refrigerator
   for at least an hour.
6. Preheat your oven to 375°F/180°C.
7. Place the chilled dough on a lightly
   floured table top, sprinkle some flour on
   top, then roll it out to about 3 mm thick.
8. Cut the dough into shapes and place on
   the baking sheet, at least 1½ cm apart.
9. Bake for 8–12 minutes or until they turn
   golden around the edges. Then remove
   from the oven and leave to cool for a few
   minutes before transferring to a wire rack.